Copyright © 2012 by David Wickey
All rights reserved. This book or any portion thereof
may not be reproduced or used in any manner whatsoever
without the express written permission of the publisher
except for the use of brief quotations in a book review.

Printed in the United States of America

First Printing, 2012

ISBN
978-1-4675-3101-6

His Way Publishing
125 N Jefferson St.
Berne, IN 46711
www.swisspress.net

## Dedication

*To my Dad, I dedicate this book. He who walked with God in such personal and intimate way. He was a man of few words but when he spoke, his words had weight.*

*One afternoon, I asked him with many questions about our faith in God. He leaned on a pitch fork for a moment and then he spoke only these words... "Ask, and it will be given to you; seek, and you will find; knock, and it will be opened to you."*

*On that day, my journey of faith had begun.*

## Publisher's Note

I first met David probably 3 years ago. I have been blessed to enjoy many interesting conversations with this man whom I have come to know as a man who is seeking God's heart and God's will.

I have seen in him a man who has a deep love and concern for the spiritual well-being of himself and people around him, especially the Amish people, who are his background.

We don't always agree on everything, as people who enjoy discussing spiritual things rarely do, since I believe everybody experiences God differently, but I believe we have learned to respect each other's opinion.

The words on the pages of this book are the record of David's spiritual journey, as well as his spiritual insights. They are from his heart. They are his opinions, and not necessarily the opinions of the publisher.

Thank-you for reading,
Wayne Schwartz
*Publisher*

## Acknowledgements

*I* want to thank my wife Chiyuki whom God has put in my life, to be my friend and my partner in the ministry of the calling God has on our lives. Thank you for leaving Phoenix and coming with me to Berne, IN where God has called us. I know it is not easy. May God bless you richly in this life and life to come!

Also I want to thank my children who have stood when things were not so good. I am so proud of you all. May God richly bless you and your mates who God has put in your lives and all the grand children. May you experience the blessings of God more and more in your lives. I love you all very much!

I want to thank my step children who also stood strong when things weren't good in your lives. I am proud of you all. May you experience the blessings of God more and more in your lives. I love you all very much!

I want to thank all the men and women God put in my life to guide me and council me in my spiritual walk with the Lord, and have ministered to me.

I want to acknowledge Pastor Glenn Foster who is with the Lord today, and all the staff members of Sweet Water Church of the Valley, where the apostles, prophets, evangelists, pastors and teachers were functioning, in whom I sat under for over twenty years. Many ministries are coming into fruition today, because of the ministry at Sweet Water Church of the Valley. Amen!

Also pastors Brian and Phaedra Alton who are also a product of Sweet Water Church of the Valley, who are now pastors of Desert Rose Community Church . Thank you for not giving up on me and recognizing the calling on our lives, and supporting us with your prayers and your ministry to us, and being our friends.

May God richly bless you!

# Foreword

*F*ull of faith, hope, and love…..full of the Holy Spirit of God. He is a man after God's own heart. He is my husband and best friend.

Last 19 years of our lives journey together, he shared his visions and his heart cries for his people and religious community until they became also mine.

In this book, he shares his childhood, family; experiences and how God took hold of him and embraced him with His love and grace.

I pray that this book will bless many and enlighten the eyes of your understanding that you may know what is the hope of His calling, what are the riches of the glory of His inheritance in the Saints; and what is the exceeding greatness of His power toward us who believe, according to the working of His mighty power which He worked in Christ when He raise Him from the dead and seated Him at His right hand in the heavenly places. (Eph. 1:18-20)

Blessings to you all,
Chiyuki Wickey

# Preface

*I* remember running the length of our fifteen acre field, from one end to the other, with my hands in the air. I felt like I was floating! It felt so good. I was eight years old when this happened, but today I know it was the Holy Spirit. He knew me before the foundation of the world!

For the last forty years I have been in school of the Holy Spirit, and I am still in this school. In this writing I will share some of the things I have learned, and have experienced through the years, from a childhood growing up, and becoming a Christian. I will share what God has worked in me concerning the Body of Jesus Christ on earth, and to build a Spiritual Temple for Him for a dwelling place for Him so His will to be done on earth as it is in Heaven.

It has been forty years now, since I have been born again. This could be just a religious phrase; being born again, to me this is reality. So I will try to share. I will not try to change anybody's mind in what they believe, but share what I have experienced. In this book I will use the name Amish, and is not meant to offend anyone. It is the way I was raised. Some of my testimony might offend some people, but it is not meant to offend anybody. It doesn't matter what name we go by , the Bible says in [Romans 3:23-24] 'For all have sinned and fall short of the glory of God, being justified freely by His grace through the redemption that is in Christ Jesus". All means everybody.

I will begin with my childhood, growing up in Adams County, Indiana, near towns called Berne and Geneva, in an Amish community.

# Chapter 1

## *My Childhood*

**W**hen I was born, my dad worked at a dairy farm. They always told me I was born in the dairy barn. Of course, that wasn't true. I was born in the house by the dairy barn. Or, maybe it was true, maybe that's why I still smell of dairy cows. Just kidding! They say you can take the boy out of the country, but you can't take the country out of the boy.

Back then, the doctor would come out to your house, and stay till the baby was born, and it didn't cost an arm and a leg to have a baby. The rest of the family had to stay in a different room until the little one was born. This was in 1944.

I have four sisters and three brothers. I am the youngest of the brothers, and I have two sisters younger than myself. Two of my brothers have passed on to be with the Lord. Dad's name was Dan, and my mother was named Mary. Both have passed on to be with the Lord.

My earliest memories of my childhood, we lived on a forty acre farm, with big hickory nut trees, with great big hickory nuts. My brother Dan and I took dad's hammers and went to the woods and cracked hickory nuts. No wonder dad could never find his tools!

We lived on a dirt road with lots of green grass on the sides of the road. I helped my older brothers watch the cows, as they grazed along the dirt road. This is called "chea hirten". Forgive me if I spelled it wrong. These were long hot days, as we watched the butterflies, and we tried to catch them and put them in jars.

I remember there were also some cold winters. One winter the snow was very deep, the top crust froze very hard. Dad walked on top of the snow to a little village called New Corydon, to get groceries. I can still see dad walking on top of the snow.

I remember one cold day; I was going with dad to the woods. My brother Dan was sick that day, and he could not go along. He was very upset. I can still see him looking out the window and crying. I felt sorry for him, but I was going to the woods with Dad! See ya later Dan. There are some things you just don't forget.

I was seven years old when Dad bought a ninety-two acre farm along Adams and Jay County line. The Wabash River flowed in the back of our property. I suppose the world could not contain all the books if it were written what happened, and what we did along the Wabash. Well, that may be stretching it a bit.

I remember my brother Dan and I were fishing one day with bamboo poles. Dan's bobber began to jerk wildly, and then took off across the water. Dan grabbed the pole, and it almost pulled him into the river. I also took hold, as the pole broke, but didn't come apart. We began pulling the pole up the bank. A big carp came flopping out of the water. We were too small to pin him down. I held unto the pole, and Dan put a bear hug around it, but couldn't hold onto the slippery fish. It flopped back into the water and took off, snapping the line in two! We stood there stunned. We should have had a camera because nobody believed our story about the whale that got away.

Can you imagine reading in the newspaper the next day "two small Amish boys catch whale in the Wabash River" with our pictures? Of course it looked like a whale to us.

My brother Dan and I spent many hours together in our barn, making tunnels in the hay. We had tunnels all over the place. I don't think the U. S. army could have found us! Actually, it's a wonder we didn't kill ourselves. We climbed all over that barn.

Recently I stopped at the old home place. The person who owns it was kind enough to give me a tour of the barn. It brought back a lot of memories.

We had a basketball goal on the side of our barn. My brother Dan and I often played basketball after school, and sometimes completely forgot to do the evening chores. We were in big trouble when dad came from work because the chores weren't done. We couldn't help it if we got carried away playing basketball, right?

As I write about my childhood I'm thinking, I had no idea what God had in store for my life, or why I was born. All I knew that I was an Amish. I was different than my English neighbors, although we had a lot of fun with the boys. We dressed different, and they had a car, and we didn't. I remember, we went to their house one day, and they had just bought a black and white TV. After this we found all kind of excuses to go to their house. That was the time we learned how to speak English. This was almost sixty years ago, I can't believe it!

One summer day, I was with my mother sitting in our front yard cleaning green beans, getting them ready to put into glass jars. We always had a basement full of canned food, meat, vegetables, and all kind of goodies. A car pulled up by our front yard. A gentleman got out of his car, and came towards us. He started talking to us about God. My mother told him that we had our own Bible, which wasn't any different from his, only ours was in German and his was in English. He didn't argue with my mother, he just raised his hands in the air, and began praying for us. As an eight year old, this was imprinted on my mind.

Of course, today I know the feeling I got while running across the field with my hands in the air was the Holy Spirit. Dear reader, you must know, God knew you before the foundation of the world. It doesn't make any difference if you're Amish, Mennonite, Baptist, or any other name. GOD IS GOD!! He is not exclusive to any of these labels we give ourselves. He had me and you in mind, when He gave His only begotten Son Jesus Christ, to die that we could live, and to know Him!![Acts 4:12] It says "Neither is there salvation in any other: for there is none other Name under heaven given among men, whereby we must be saved.]

When I was fifteen years old, I became ill. I was always hungry and thirsty, and kept losing weight. I was diagnosed as a type one diabetic. I must mention this, because it played a big part in my Christian walk in shaping me for His Glory. In the following chapters this will be mentioned some more.

In the following chapter, I will write about my early adult life in the Amish church, and my testimony, how I met Jesus Christ. This is not to offend anybody, but like Paul the Apostle, told his testimony, how he met Jesus Christ. It is good to testify about the life of Christ in us!

# Chapter 2

## My Empty Heart

*I* got baptized into the Amish church when I was seventeen, according to the tradition of the Amish church. We didn't believe in baptizing babies. We had to learn eighteen articles of the faith, in German of course. For me this was all head knowledge, not from the heart, though the words were good, but for me everything pointed to the Amish church, And not to Jesus by Faith. At that time my faith was in the Amish church and not in Jesus, because of our outward separation from what I thought was worldly. I was just as much worldly after I was baptized as I was before I was baptized, but now I could participate in church affairs, in taking communion, and foot washing. For me, everything was just a form I went through, without knowing Jesus by a living Faith that comes from God. I didn't know this because I was not taught this. All I was taught was the Amish lifestyle of rules and regulations, and this is so sad. The outward was keeping me from the inward, in other words keeping me from knowing Jesus. Yes we can become like the Pharisees and Scribes without realizing it. God, bring us back to the Living Faith!

I remember two weeks after I got baptized, the deacon of the church took me aside, and talked to me about my hair. He thought it was too short. We were supposed to have a certain length, not too short, and not too long. My mother gave me a haircut after I was baptized, and cut it on the short side. The deacon told me to be careful. Do you see the deception of the outward versus the inward? I actually thought that God was Amish, and Jesus was Amish, too, and if I followed all the rules, there might be a hope that I could go to Heaven some day.

Today as I see the Amish, many are recognizing this deception. My dear brothers and sisters, you can let go of these outward worldly things, and come to Jesus by GRACE THROUGH FAITH. It will set you free to know Christ in a new and living way. The Holy Spirit will not deceive you! Do not fear men, or what men think, come to Him like a little child, and hear Him! He will reveal Himself to you. It's that simple! We as humans, and our way of thinking, makes it so hard. We start to think what kind of cloth I should wear on my head, or if I should wear one at all, or how big of a hat I should wear, or if I should wear one at all. This kind of thinking will never bring us into the life of Christ! Never, never! It is like giving in to Satan, when he came to Eve in the garden, and the Lord God commanded the man, saying, of every tree of the garden thou may freely eat: but of the tree of the knowledge of good and evil, thou shall not eat of it: for in the day that thou eats there of thou shall surely die. And the serpent said unto the woman, you shall not surely die: for God doth know that in the day you eat there of, then your eyes shall be opened, and you shall be as gods, knowing good and evil". My friends, this is where all man made doctrine comes from, and brings forth death. Let's become like a little child and just simply trust Jesus. He will teach us! Let's start eating from the tree of LIFE that has so freely been given to us by GRACE THROUGH FAITH that is in JESUS CHRIST and not of our own self righteousness!!

I just wanted to work, and make a living, and live a good satisfied life, but as time went on I became very dissatisfied. I had a brother-in-law that didn't follow the rules very well. He was excommunicated more than he belonged to the church. I always got in trouble, because I didn't shun him. I couldn't shun him, because I didn't feel like I was better than him. At the same time, there was much confusion in my life, with my empty heart. I was just plain miserable. When I didn't shun someone that I was supposed to shun, I always felt condemned, and lived in guilt.

I hated conflict, and there was plenty of conflict in the church I was a member in at that time. So, in 1969, I rebelled against the church I was in, and left. I sold my horse and buggy, and bought a 1959 Star Chief Pontiac, and started dressing in English clothes. We had our house wired for electricity, and even bought a black and white TV. None of these things could satisfy me.

I loved Blue Grass music, and still do. We had some beer parties, and invited musicians to come and play, and of course drink all the beer they wanted, but I still had an empty heart, and was very miserable. If I had known about drugs I would have probably tried them.

My life was in a very confused state, and I was feeling condemned all time. My heart still so empty, and my family shunning me, because they thought I was living the high life, instead of the "lowly" life, as required by the church. I know now, that the lifestyle of the church I came out of was not lowly at all, but at the time, I thought that I had to go back to it. I decided to humble myself, and confess all my high or worldly living. I went to the Amish ministers and confessed as much as I knew how. I sold my car and bought a horse and buggy, and had the electric company turn off our electricity. I was trying to fill my empty heart, this time by trying to please men. This will make you feel better for a while, because it will please your family and the church where you attend. It is like putting a band aid over your heart, and not coming to the root of the problem. I did not know that you have to be BORN AGAIN, and the ministers of my home church did not know this either. They used the phrase [born again] but everything pointed to the Church, and their way of life. They say, if your heart is right you will obey the rules of the Church, and not cause any problem, and this is deception. It is like Satan coming as an angel of light. He always comes in religious forms, and voids the life of Christ. This is eating from tree of the knowledge of good and evil.

I tried to obey as much as I knew how. The harder I tried the emptier I became. The band aid was coming off. I was a very miserable man, very empty and and confused. I remember in those days; I went home to visit my dad, because I was feeling so miserable. I stayed home from work to go see him. Life just didn't make any sense.

Dad was cleaning the horse stable when I got there, so I picked up a fork and helped him. Questions began pouring out of me. Dad was a man of few words. He searched the Scriptures himself in German. I believe he also had an empty heart. When I was finished, he looked at me and said, "The Bible says, 'Ask, and it shall be given you; seek, and you shall find; knock, and it shall be opened unto you'." He didn't say any more. He didn't lecture me about all of the outward things. He gave me the best counsel for me at that time. But I still didn't know what to do about my empty heart.

One evening, as I was doing my evening chores, it all came to a head. I was by a wagon in the barn, and the wagon tongue was in front of me. I knelt by the wagon tongue and for the first time in my life I started crying out to God from depth of my being; "God I know that You are. I don't care if it is Amish or what it is, I need YOU, help me!"

It was the first time I ever prayed like that, from my heart. I had always prayed out of a prayer book before. This was different. This was a complete surrender to the living God. A God that is, but can't be seen with your natural eye, because God is Spirit! My inner man was BORN AGAIN! I felt the presence of holy angels all around me! I became His possession! Although I really didn't know what happened to me at that time, I knew I was changed, and my empty heart became very excited; this was very new to me. I wasn't taught this in the church I was in a member of. I was so hungry for the word of God! I began reading the Bible in English. I ate the word of God, and it tasted so good! [John 3:3-8]

# Chapter 3
## Signs from God

*Therefore if any man be in Christ, he is a new creature: old things are passed away; behold all things are become new"*. [2 Corinthians 5:17]

I never knew I could have a personal relationship with Jesus Christ by the power of the Holy Spirit. In those days I learned how to talk to Him, and it was so precious, and still is today! My beloved friends, it is so simple, if it would take a smart person that can solve all problems, and make all the correct decisions, none of us would qualify to be Christians.

Why do we set up a bunch of rules and regulations, and not trust the Holy Spirit to teach us? I believe we are still eating from the tree of the knowledge of good and evil. Yes, it makes us feel good for a while, but in the end it brings forth death, and not life. Let's eat from the TREE OF LIFE BY GRACE THROUGH FAITH! It is a gift! We are all invited to eat from this table, the table of the Lord! It doesn't cost any money, and it lasts forever!

I did not keep these things quiet in those days. I also did not have much wisdom in those days. I was like a young calf that was born in the winter time, and when spring came was put out in the open fields, and running wildly into fences. I was running into fences all the time. Like Moses in the Bible, I did more harm than good sometimes! But God put people in my life that walked this way before I did, to lead me, and help me. You can read this in the Bible, about men and women of God which are over you in the Lord. Perhaps after forty years, I could write another book on this subject.

My Mother, not understanding, said I had met the devil in my barn experience. Of course, I was very offended. One of the men of God that God had put in my life said, "David, you must forgive your Mother."

Because of this, I forgave her in my heart. Thank God before she died, there was peace between us. Some times dear reader, we look on the outward, and don't know what's going on in the inward, and speak of what we see, and misinterpret the situation. We are all guilty of this and many offenses come through this. We must forgive each other. The man of God could have said, "Yes, David your Mother was very wrong, and you are right, and you must tell her she is wrong." This would have been the wrong advice, and would have caused more strife. He just simply said that I must forgive her.

The Amish ministers heard about the things that were happening to me, and came to visit me. I was informed that they were coming Wednesday evening. When I saw them coming down the road with the horse and buggy, I went into my coal shed, where I often went to pray and talk to God. I prayed, "Jesus, they are coming down the road, (as if He didn't know!) and I don't know what to tell them so I give this situation to You."

I invited them to come into the house. They began to ask a lot of questions concerning what I believed. I answered the best I knew how. What could I say, except that I had been born again? They didn't believe in being born again, except by being baptized into the Amish church. They didn't believe that you could be born again in a barn, and know Jesus in a very intimate and personal way. The Bishop said that my case was a very difficult case.

At that time we had talked about moving to Arizona. I just wanted to move away from the conflict with family and the Amish church. One of the ministers said, "We heard you are going to move to Arizona."

I answered and said, "We have talked about it, but the Lord will lead you if you let Him." I didn't know the power of those words! When I spoke those words, there was a noise, and our house shook where we were sitting. The minister asked what that was. I answered him truthfully, and said, " I don't know."
I remember looking out the window to see if there was anything outside, but there wasn't. The ministers left the house after this happened.

I went downstairs to our basement to check the flooring and all the doors, but nothing was out of order. As I came back upstairs,

I felt that familiar presences as in the barn experience. Dear reader, Jesus is so near to us even in our mouth. [Romans10:8] What does it mean to be led by the Holy Spirit? [Romans8:14]; for as many as are led by the Spirit of God, they are the sons of God". What does it mean to be a son of God?

At a later time in the same house, I was sitting in my rocking chair, reading the Bible. I was reading in the Gospel of John, and I came to chapter 14, verse26."But the Comforter, which is the Holy Ghost, whom the Father will send in my name, He shall teach you all things, and bring all things to your remembrance, whatsoever I have said unto you". When I read this verse, the Holy Spirit took hold of my physical body, and I could not move, and the Scripture came out of the Bible at me. I don't know how long I sat there until I could move again.

This is a reminder to you who say, the Bible was written by the opinions of man. The Bible is the living word of God, it is alive! It is not just another book, and the Holy Spirit will teach us how to interpret the Holy Word of God.

Why was God sending these signs in my life? It was because of the situation I was in at that time, and He has a plan for my life, and I was to remember these, as I would go through His dealings in my life, to bring me out of myself, and into Him. He changes my way of thinking and into His way of thinking. [1Corinthians2:14-16].

In those days I wanted to make my family, and the Amish church to understand what had happened to me, and that God was with me. In chapter one, I mentioned I became a Type 1 diabetic at the age of fifteen, and so without asking God, I decided to stop taking insulin to prove to them that God was with me, and God would heal me. Then they would know that God was with me. How foolish! About a week later I became very ill, and they had to take me to the hospital. That night I was so sick I thought I was going to die. The Doctors were very graceful, and didn't ask too many questions. They started giving me insulin again. I was so humiliated, and couldn't pray until the day I left the hospital. I went to the hospital sanctuary, and as I was starting to kneel down, the Holy Spirit spoke to me, and said,

"It's alright my son!" God never condemns, but always leads, because we are His children, sons and daughters!

I don't have to prove to any one that God is with me. God will do that. By the way, I am sixty seven years old now, and I have no complications of diabetes at all, and I won't have either. Somebody might ask, don't you believe in divine healing? Yes I do, but in God's way and, in God's time. God had a much bigger plan than me not taking insulin, or proving to somebody that God was with me. Much more could be written on healing. By the way, if you are believing God to heal diabetes, He will do it. Many have been supernaturally healed of this condition. Again much could be written on this subject. It is all about the Kingdom of God on earth, and the calling that's on a person's life. I remember in the Amish church they did what they called braucha. This is not God's way of healing, and is very dangerous. God heals the healthy way, and in the knowledge of Him, and what He did for us on the cross of His great love for us, and it is not spooky.

## Chapter 4

### The True Foundation

**D**own through years, God has given me dreams and visions. This is one way He speaks to us. If we are to be led by Him, we have to hear from Him. He speaks to us in many different ways, and dreams and visions are ways He speaks to us. Examples in the Bible are found in Acts 2:17, Acts 10:3, Acts 16:9, and many, many more, in the Old Testament and the new. God still speaks in this way. Some times He speaks directly to our spirit by the Holy Spirit. Again many things could be written on this subject.

In 1974, God gave me a dream. In this dream some Christian brothers and I were building a building on a foundation that was already there. What we were doing was very accurate and precise, and it felt so good. You builders out there know what I'm talking about. As we were working, I heard somebody in the back ground shouting FIRE, FIRE. I looked, and there was my mother and my sister standing by a building, and the foundation was on fire. I thought to myself I must help them put out their fire. There was a horse tank nearby, and I took a bucket and started taking water out of the horse tank, and pouring water on the fire. The more water I poured on the fire, the more it burned, until it was completely burned up. This dream can be found in 1 Corinthians Chapter 3.

What was this dream about? When a person dreams a dream from God, it is usually about the person that dreamed the dream, and this person must live that dream. If we have a dream from the Lord, we must seek God for the interpretation. Sometimes a brother or sister in Christ will interpret the dream, and sometimes you just have to wait on the Lord, and He will give us understanding as we live it.

I believe the foundation my Christians brothers and I were

building on was Jesus Christ. [I Corinthians 3: 11] For other foundation can no man lay than that is laid, which is Jesus Christ]. What kind of foundation was burning where my mother and sister were standing? God is burning my foundation that was not Jesus Christ. What was the horse tank for? A horse represents the strength of man, and not God. [Psalm 33: 16-22] [Psalm 20: 7]. Also I was raised with horse and buggies. The water that I was pouring on the fire was coming from the wrong source. It was coming from the strength of man.

When we become Born Again, our inner man becomes Born Again. We are than on the true foundation, but to build on it is another story, because we have layers and layers of outer selfish flesh that has to be burned up. This has happened and is happening in my life, but the good news is, the more we decrease, or are burned up, the more He increases in our lives. Let's let the fire burn! We than can do the will of God on earth as it is in Heaven! My friends, this is true Christianity! This is the straight and narrow! This will bring us into the eternal life of Christ. *I indeed baptize you with water unto repentance: but he that cometh after me is mightier than I, He shall baptize you with the Holy Ghost, and with FIRE: whose fan is in His hand, and He will thoroughly purge His floor, and gather His wheat into the garner; but He will burn up the chaff with unquenchable FIRE.[Matthew3:11-12 KJV]*

God does all this with His great LOVE for us. The work comes from God's side and not from our side. The more that Holy fire burns, the more we will know Him and His ways and thoughts. We will begin to get His mind. This is called holiness, and without holiness we will not see the Lord! This is why we must have the apostles, prophets, evangelists, and pastors and teachers, functioning in the body of Christ, for the perfecting of the saints, or to bring us into maturity. Till we all come in the unity of the Faith, and the knowledge of the Son of God, into a perfect man, unto the measure of the stature of the fullness of Christ. [Ephesians chapter 4] I will write some more on this subject in chapter 7 and 8 of this book. Because the body of Christ is so dear to my heart, and burns in my spirit, and should be in every born again believer. Because it is the CHRIST we are contending with, and not doctrines of men.

I remember in one of my lowest times in my life. I had lost all hope, it seemed like I had lost everything. I had failed God so much, and I could never have fellowship with Him again. I had gone to a prayer meeting, one Friday evening in the church. People came and left as they pleased. The church was open to everybody. I was sitting by myself in a dark corner. I was just sitting there not praying and not trying to pray. Not expecting it, the Holy Spirit began speaking to my spirit, and this is what He said; "Humpty Dumpty sat on a wall, Humpty Dumpty had a great fall. All the kings' horses and all the kings' men couldn't put humpty back together again... but I can!"
   He filled me with a baptism of love right there, sitting in a dark corner by myself. I just sat there and cried. My dear brothers and sisters it is so good just to fall in His arms of His great love! When I sit in darkness the Lord will be a light unto me.
   A religious person might say; God doesn't speak to you like that. All I can say you have never experienced the dealings of God, and have never experienced His Great LOVE. I was not thinking of nursery rhymes at that time in my life. We do have to come to Him like a little child. He takes our strength away, and gives us His. It's a gift! Remember, Jesus never condemns, but leads us out of darkness into His marvelous light! We are partakers of His divine nature! It is called Jesus Christ and Him crucified! THE CROSS OF LOVE!

# Chapter 5

## The Love of God

**W**hen I speak about the people called Amish, is because I was raised this way, and my love for this people is great. I love them and so does God. It is in my heart to write what I have experienced down through the years, for edification, and not to condemn anybody. *Beloved, let us love one another, for love is of God; and everyone who loves is born of God and knows God.* [1John4:7-8 NKJV]

As I said before, God has given me dreams and visions through the years. In 2006 I had a dream, and in this dream I had a visitation from God. In my dream a preacher was preaching about the awesome love of God, as I was listening, and I was thinking to myself, this is not for me. I am not worthy of this great love it must be for somebody else. As I was thinking this way, a bubble of LOVE went around me. This is the only way I can explain it. It can not be put into human words. My wife was also in the dream. It was like He could visit every human being at anytime in the whole world. "*What is man that You are mindful of him, and the son of man that You visit him*". [ Psalm 8:4 NKJV]

He came to me personally, my background being Old Order Amish, He knows my burden for this religious people, who do many good works, but there may be some who do not know the awesome LOVE of GOD, or know Him personally, because they try to save themselves by good works, and not by the finished work of GRACE, and they don't know they are doing this.

Also in this bubble of this HOLY LOVE, I saw this Amish couple, which I didn't recognize. This couple was experiencing the same LOVE I was experiencing. I saw the gentleman looking in his Bible, saying is this LOVE in the Bible? It was so new to him.

He thought it might deceive him, and the preacher who is the Lord spoke to him; yes this is in the Bible. We were all in this awesome presence of HOLY LOVE! *"For God so loved the world that He gave His only begotten Son, that whoever believes in Him should not perish but have everlasting life"*.[John 3:16 NKJV]

As I started to come out of this visitation, I fought to stay in it, but I could not. I didn't know where I was . Our night light was shining on our ceiling fan, and it made a shadow of a cross. This was the first thing I saw as I came out of this visitation. This cross is not to condemn people, but to save people! *For God did not send His Son into the world to condemn the world, but that the world through Him might be saved."* [John3:17} This includes all people, Amish, Mennonite, black, white, brown, yellow, red, the drunk, the one that never misses a church service, the liberal, the conservative, the plain people, and the non plain people, the Jew, the Gentile, the drug addict, the homeless, the millionaire, ALL PEOPLE!

Since my wife was in this visitation, I thought she knew all about it. She woke up and asked me what was wrong. I told her I had a visitation from God! I sat there and cried like a baby. My dear friends GOD IS LOVE! What good is it to be a Christian if we don't know the LOVE OF GOD! I can't save myself with my own good works. O wretched man that I am! Who will deliver me from this body of death? I thank God-through Jesus Christ our Lord! So then, I myself serve the law of God, but with the flesh the law of sin. There is now no condemnation to those who are in Christ Jesus, who do not walk according to the flesh, but according to the Spirit. For the law of the Spirit of life in Christ Jesus has made me free from the law of sin and death .AMEN!! Please read the book of Romans with spiritual understanding of the love of God.

All it takes is to come like a child, and to trust Him to bring us into His salvation, and into a Love relationship with Him. My friends, it is so easy. *"Come to me, all you who labor and are heavy laden, and I will give you rest. Take My yoke upon you and learn of Me, for I am gentle lowly in heart, and you will find rest in your souls. For My yoke is easy and My burden is light.* [Matthew11:28-30 NKJV]

# Chapter 6

## The Perfect Law of Liberty

*T*he book of James is a very interesting book. It speaks about the perfect law of liberty, and faith without works is dead. Paul in Ephesians says we are saved by grace through faith and not by works lest we should boast. So who is correct, Paul or James? They are both correct. To really understand these books we must go through the dealings of God or in other words let that fire burn. I call it the school of the Holy Spirit, or being led by God. How can layers of stinking flesh do good works? All it will amount to is to bring glory to self, and bring lots and lots of false humility. It will bring forth many false doctrines, and cause many divisions in the Body of Christ. So where does the work come in?

The Bible says judgment starts in the house of God. When God starts judging those layers of stinking flesh, not to destroy us, but to save us, the works start. What is faith for, if it does not have works that saves us? Faith standing alone and not working is a dead faith, and is good for nothing, and we stay in our own sin nature. We are saved by Grace through faith; and that not of ourselves: it is a gift of God: Not of works, lest any man should boast. For we are His workmanship, created in Christ Jesus unto good works, which God hath before ordained that we should walk in these good works. Salvation always comes from God's side, and not from us. It is a gift! We become partakers of it.

My, my, this is good news! This work that Faith does allows us to become a doer of the word, and not a hearer only. To do the will of God, we must first allow His will to be worked out in us, or allowing Him to lead us. Young people hear this word. Our problem is we want to put the buggy before the horse. There is a divine order in being a son or daughter of God and it is God's order. The good news is He doesn't throw us away when we mess up. He brings us out of darkness into His Light. There is now no condemnation to them which are in Christ Jesus, who walk not after the flesh, but after the Spirit.

What is this perfect law of liberty? It is the new covenant of Grace and Truth, and not under the old covenant law. We are no longer judged by the law of the old covenant, which brings death, but we are judged by grace, the new covenant, which is the perfect law of liberty, and it brings us into eternal life. GOD IS LOVE!! IT IS A GIFT!! If somebody paid all your dept that you owe, and one day you went to the bank, and they said somebody paid your mortgage in full, and not only that, there is one million dollars in your bank account. It would be hard for us to believe this, because we didn't work for it, or earn it. That is why it is so hard for us to receive the free gift of Salvation. We think we have to earn it, and many denominations were started on this foundation, which is the wrong foundation. It is still eating from the tree of the knowledge of good and evil.

Remember when our house shook, when I said the Lord will lead you if you let Him? This is what God had in mind, to bring me out of my ignorance, and into His Salvation, and He has this in mind for the Amish, the Mennonite, the Baptist, the Methodist, the Lutheran, the Pentecostal, and every other name you can think of. There is one body, and one Spirit, even as we are called in one hope of our calling; One Lord, one Faith, one baptism, one God and Father of all, and through all, and in you all. You can find this in Ephesians chapter four. Let's not be divided but united in that free Gift of salvation. All it takes is a divine humility, coming as a little child, coming to a place where I know nothing; I can do nothing, and crying out to God for His wisdom, let's not be ashamed of the good news of Jesus Christ. If I don't humble myself now, there will come a day I will be humbled. It's in the Bible, and this is not good news!

In 2005, my wife and I traveled to Israel with a group, and there were people from different churches, and denominations in our group. I became friends with a Lutheran brother. We were all interested in things we saw in the Holy Land, where Jesus walked when He was still on this earth. All of Christianity stems from Jesus Christ, and His crucifixion, and resurrection. I asked this Lutheran brother if he thinks the churches and denominations will ever unite, and be one. He said he doesn't think so. He said there would have to be too much compromise. How sad this is. I don't know what he meant by that. The only thing I could think of, we interpret or misinterpret the bible in different ways, and that brings me to the next chapter of this book. I do believe the Holy Spirit is bringing more and more unity in the church. Again, it takes great humility, and that is not compromising in what we believe, but it is submitting to the KING OF KINGS AND the LORD OF LORDS, by HIS grace and HIS faith in us, then we will not try to come into unity, but we will be in unity! CHRIST IS NOT DIVIDED!!

## Chapter 7

### The Body of Christ

**W**hen we think of church, what do we think about? Do we think of some building, and a pastor standing behind a podium, and giving sermons? Maybe he is speaking about the things that are wrong in our country, and telling people to become better people. This is good, but it isn't what God has intended for the church to be. What is our first thought when we think about church? Maybe you have been terribly hurt in church, and want nothing to do with what you think is Christianity, or maybe you are like I was, being taught the rules of what you could have and not have, and what is worldly and not worldly, and how you should dress. Maybe the first thing you think about is money, and you don't want to have anything to do with church, because they are always asking for money. In this last chapter I want to pour out my heart, of what I think, and what I have experienced on this subject of church.

First of all church is not a building, or what we think is a church house, and it is not a pastor behind a podium giving sermons and feeling good about ourselves, and it is not a bunch of rules and regulations, what is right and what is wrong and what is worldly and not worldly. I have already written in this book, many things I have experienced, but I want to go a little deeper in this area, because I think it is the most important operation we have going on earth today, THE BODY OF CHRIST! It is not the economy, it is not health care, or anything like that. It is the LIVING ORGANISM OF JESUS CHRIST ON EARTH BY THE PERSON OF THE HOLY SPIRIT DWELLING IN HIS MEMBERS.

This is what affects everything, from our personal lives, and our families, and our communities, and our State, and our country, and the world, even the physical earth we live on. Please read scripture references. [Genesis 3:17-19] [Romans 8:18-22]. Remember the Bible is the living word of God, and can't be understood except by the Holy Spirit that abides in us. [1 Corinthians 2: 11-16].

After having said these things, what do I do? I want to help build a building where Jesus Christ is the foundation, a house where He can come and dwell in. Who are the people qualified to work on this building?

Recently while watching TV, I believe it was on a Christian channel, Reinhart Bonnke, an evangelist from Germany who preaches in Africa was teaching some young people. He was saying, when he was 8 years old, they were having a missionary meeting, with his dad who was a missionary to Africa. The Holy Spirit spoke to his heart, and said, "You will preach in Africa."

He was very excited, and told his dad. His dad said, "No my son it will be your oldest brother that will be my successor." His dad thought the older brother was better equipped for the job. Reinhard went on to say, in Germany, when somebody was looked down upon, or did not have a good reputation, he or she was called a zero or in German a *null*. He went on to say, when Jesus had prayed all night in choosing who should be His disciples, it would seem He would have gone to the University of Jerusalem, and chose the best of the best, the ones that people would choose. He didn't do that. He started choosing zeros.

Do you feel like a zero? Do you feel like you don't fit in any place, maybe you have been rejected by family or church, or whatever the case, you just feel like a zero. You are the one that Jesus has chosen to help build this house. You might feel like you have done to many bad things, and you're not worthy. You are the one Jesus has chosen, come and follow Him. He will put you to work building this house for Him to dwell in. No experience necessary. It is on the job training, and the pay is eternal life, to know Him and the power of His resurrection in this life and the life to come! Yes, He will make us fishers of men.

*Now, therefore, you are no longer strangers and foreigners, but fellow citizens with the household of God, having been built on the foundation of the apostles and prophets, Jesus Christ Himself being THE chief cornerstone fitted together, grows into a holy temple in the Lord, in whom you also are being built together for a dwelling place of God in the Spirit.* [Ephesians2:19-22] Paul is talking to Gentiles, who were not a people of God like the Jews, but were called to grow into a Holy temple in the Lord. If there was ever a zero it was a Gentile, and we are Gentiles.

What is going to solve our personal problems, our community problems, our nation's problems, and the world's problems? I know this is a hard word, but it is true. It is the people of God, or the Body of Jesus Christ on earth that have to become what we were called to be. The Kingdom of God to come on earth as it is in Heaven this was always God's will since the fall where we gave in to the scheme of Satan.

In 2 Chronicles, Solomon had built the Temple, a house God could dwell in. It was in Solomon's heart to build this house. Today it should be in the hearts of God's people, the Body of Christ, to build a spiritual house for Jesus to come live in, and I might add not just wait for the rapture. Today we are the Temple of the Holy Spirit! It starts in our personal lives first. *I am the temple of the Holy Spirit!* [1Corinthians3:16]. If it is not in our hearts to do this, and we just want to do our own thing, maybe have our own ministries, and think we can do something on our own, then I believe we need to implement the scripture in When I shut up heaven and there is no rain, or command the locusts to devour the land, or send pestilence among my people, if my people who are called by My Name will humble themselves, and pray and seek My face, and turn from their wicked ways, then I will hear from heaven, and will forgive their sin and heal their land". 2Chronicles7:13-14

When I was Amish, when somebody did something that went against the Amish rules we had to confess to the ministers and to the Amish congregation what we did wrong, and it went something like this, I confess I sinned against God and His church, and I will try to do better. This can be like putting a band aid on your heart, and not going to the root of the problem, which can only be healed by the finished work of GRACE that Jesus did for us, that pure Holy Blood was shed for us, and we don't have to save ourselves anymore. This is what is called being a member of His Body, and letting HIM baptize us with the Holy Spirit and fire. Then we can begin to build on the true foundation, which is Jesus Christ. Any other way is a wicked way. *We are saved by grace through faith, and not of ourselves; it is a gift of God, not of works, lest anyone should boast.* [Ephesians 2:8-9]

This is truly humbling ourselves and seeking Him. Again, we become like a little child, knowing nothing. It is like a slate that has been wiped clean, than He begins to write on our slates His ways, and His thoughts. He gives us the revelation of Himself. And not some dead doctrine of some church. He is our living doctrine! He grows us up to be a building where He can come and dwell in! He is the architect of the house! He brings us out of darkness into His marvelous light. Than we will begin to be partakers of His divine nature, and we will have Holy fellowship with each other. This is when things will start to change in our lives, in our communities, and in our nation. [Matthew5:13-16]

*Let us not be divided, but let us be united in building so He can come and dwell in His Temple. Then we will experience the same thing they experienced in Solomon's day.* [Acts2:2] Yes we are going to experience this in the days and years ahead, as we continue to build His house, where He can come and dwell in.

Then we no longer play church, but we will be the church. It is called the LIVING BODY OF JESUS CHRIST ON EARTH BY THE POWER OF THE HOLY SPIRIT IN US! This will change our communities, our cities, our Nation, and the world. It is not by might or by power, but by the Holy Spirit!

# Chapter 8

*Ed. Note: We have heard since the time of this writing that the government of Myanmar has become more open to Christinaity, allowing the church there to worship much more openly.*

### Unity in Myanmar

**M**y wife, Chiyuki and I were privileged to travel to the former country of Burma, now called Myanmar with a team, our Pastors from Desert Rose Community Church, and a singing group called Treasure from Phoenix, AZ.

We had traveled to the Philippines to attend an international conference, where we met a Pastor from Myanmar. He invited us to come and help them. They needed help in financial, physical and spiritual areas.

Myanmar is a militarily controlled government. It is not like America, where you can voice your opinions. It was a few months before, when the Monks protested against the government, and many were killed. We stayed at a hotel near where this happened.

When this happens in a country, the church or the Body of Christ becomes more Christ centered, or in unity in the things of God. We foreigners should not bring our man made doctrines in, but bring Christ in Spirit and Truth. To bring in anything else besides Christ and by the power of the Holy Spirit causes confusion and disunity. The same is true in any country, including America. What love, what power, what teachings and all the gifts of the Holy Spirit come forth in these kinds of gatherings!! May we experience this more and more.

All church buildings are owned by the government. The church where we held our main meetings was a Baptist building, owned by the government. Many came from different churches and groups. We did not have any interference from the government. God did many wonderful things in those meetings, including physical healings. We did hear of others that had ministered in this country, and were heavily fined for preaching the Gospel.

They are a very needy people. Many eat only one meal a day

and eat what they can find. You don't see very many overweight people. My heart went out to them. We all felt so helpless. We did help what we could, including preparing a box with shoes and many other things. One lady had been praying for a certain pair of shoes. One of the ladies on our team had packed a pair of shoes just what the lady from Myanmar had been praying for. She was overjoyed! I believe my friends; we should visit in a country like Myanmar, and see how people's lives are controlled by an evil selfish government. I pray America is spared from this. I pray the church becomes the church what God intended for her to be.

They have a Bible school, and they showed us where the students lived. I can't begin to describe the conditions they lived in, but the hunger for the Word of God is greater than then these conditions!

We were invited by the pastor from Myanmar to attend their services. There meetings were held in an upstairs apartment, and as we went up the stair way I noticed the walls were in need of repair, but the room where the meeting was held was very clean. As we sat down I noticed a taped up guitar and a keyboard, which they used to worship the Lord with. As the meeting started, and we began to sing praises unto God, and the Holy Spirit was there to minister to us. Our pastor from Arizona had a message of comfort and edifying the Body of Christ.

My dear brothers and sisters where Jesus is, there is Unity and refreshing in the Holy Spirit, no matter the color of skin or how we are dressed. The Holy Spirit gifts are in operation, and the Love of God is understood, and man's opinions are washed away. This is beautiful to behold!! [ Psalm 133]"Behold, how good and how pleasant it is, for "brethren to dwell together in unity! It is like the precious oil upon the head, running down the beard, the beard of Aaron. Running down on the edge of his garments. It is like the dew of"Hermon, Descending upon the mountains of Zion. For "there the Lord commanded the blessing- life forevermore. [NKJ].

To come into this kind of worship in the Spirit and in Truth, also in our daily lives, there is a work that must take place in our lives, as we submit in humility, to the working of the Holy Spirit in our lives, as we allow Him to change our thinking into His thinking. It is called repentance. I will write scripture references at this time to explain this. [Isaiah: 55: 6-9] [Matthew3:1-3] [1 Corinthians: 2: 11-16] [Ephesians: 2: 7-10], and many more Scriptures. The Prophets of old prophesied this. John the Baptist prophesied this. Jesus Himself taught us this. The Holy Spirit today still teaches us the same, as we humble ourselves and allow Him to teach, and take us from our thinking into His thinking, as He works in us by His power, and by His Love! Then we will know the Truth, and knowing this truth, will make us FREE!!

    Let's it first start in our own lives, then in our communities. My friends it's time. He wants to come and dwell among united believers. [2Chronicles6:18] "But will God indeed dwell with men on the earth? Behold heaven and the heaven of heavens cannot contain You. How much less this temple which I have built!"[Rev22:20] He who testifies to these things says,"SURELY I AM COMING QUICKLY." Amen. Even so, come, LORD JESUS!

## End Note

When I was twenty six years old, I had an encounter with Jesus Christ In my barn. After forty years of being a Christian, I can only say, I am what I am by the grace of God. I am not any better than the worst sinner in the world. Knowing this I also know that is why He died on the cross, taking all my sin upon Him, and setting me free from the bondage of sin and destruction, and giving me His strength to overcome all of Satan's attacks. And giving me His mind and His life if I so choose Him. WHAT LOVE!!

To the Amish who might be reading this writing, I love you and Jesus loves you. If He didn't love you I wouldn't be writing this writing, and I would be doing my own thing. There are some hard sayings in this writing, as I have said in the preface it is not intended to offend anyone. It is what I have experienced down through years, and like Paul the Apostle says" For I neither received it from man, nor was I taught it, but it came through revelation of Jesus Christ" [ Galatians :1-12].

                      God bless you all!

     David Wickey          carpenterdavid805@gmail.com
     602-448-8528